The BIG BOOK of Grandparents' Names

With over 1,000 names for grandparents in English
plus even more in 200 languages

JEANMARIE O'KEEFE-MOORE

SILVER HALO PRESS

ISBN: 978-0-615-29017-1

Silver Halo Press
1093 A1A Beach Blvd, PMB 233
St. Augustine, FL 32080

silverhalopress.com
email: silverhalopress@gmail.com

Book design by Valerie Lentz Horowitz
Cover design by Kati Fahey

Printed in the United States of America on acid-free paper

Dedication

To my precious and beautiful grandchildren Natalie and Brody, you have truly blessed my life. You were the inspiration for your "Mimi" writing this book. I just love being your "Mimi." You have me wrapped around your tiny fingers! I love you with all my heart and soul.

Special Dedication

To my father, James O'Keefe, you are the world's greatest father and "Pop Pop" to your grandchildren. You have always been my biggest fan. I am eternally grateful for your love, encouragement and support and all your nudging for me to write this book. I love you Daddy!

Acknowledgments

Words can not begin to express my gratitude to the following:

Valerie Lentz Horowitz. I could not have done this without you. Your talents amaze me, your enthusiasm and support got me through each and every bump. Sharing and caring about all the things happening in my life. The countless hours away from your own family and hard work to dedicate to this book was more than I expected or deserved. You did it all out of the kindness of your heart. I have gained a wealth of priceless knowledge from you. Your passion is an inspiration to me. You really put your heart into this and I can't express my gratitude. I am your biggest fan. I am so blessed to have you in my life my new big sister. Thank you is not enough. We did it!

My awesome family for all your unbendable love, faith, hope, courage, strength and support to succeed despite any obstacles I face. You were there through all the ups and downs, inspiring and giving me the drive to "Just Do It." I love you!

Barbara "Cookie" Smith. You have made this all possible. You have supported and cheered me on, handled so many tasks, reminded me to slow down when I needed to rest, built and decorated my own little writing sanctuary, filled me with laughter and have kept me sane. I have lost track how many times you said to me, "It's all going to work out, just have faith." You have worked diligently and tirelessly in every aspect of this project. You are more than a best friend, you are my family. You were there through it all, and we both have the phone bills to prove it. I love you Cookster!!

Robert "Buddha Bob" Quinn. You are living proof that Angels are among us in this world. I have yet to meet you, but that will change soon. Your faith, support and resources that you so generously shared with me touches my soul. You are a rare breed and it will be an honor for me to give you the world's biggest hug. God Bless you!

Acknowledgments

● ●

To the published authors and mentors that have shown me the ropes. I am proud to join you in this crazy, wonderful literary world. It would have taken me years to gain the knowledge you shared with me. Thank you for helping my learn how to fly.

To my wonderful friends, each of you has taken an active role to help me accomplish my dream. Offering support and help with anything I needed. You have kept me motivated and your excitement has been so contagious. Writing can be very isolating at times. Thank you for being here, dragging me away from the computer and out into the world. I would be a hermit without you.

To my "MS" Sisters, I can not begin to thank you for all the help, advice, phone calls, emails, healing thoughts and prayers. You are all such a strong and brave bunch of friends. Writing this book is for all of us who suffer with Multiple Sclerosis. It shows the world that "We have MS but MS doesn't have us." Your strength and positive attitude continue to inspire me everyday!

To my beautiful children Punkin, Jillie and Chris, you are by far my biggest and best accomplishment. Nothing has been more rewarding than being your mother. There is no love like a mother feels for her child, except ot course how a grandparent feels about their grandchild. Writing this book bought back so many memories of when you all were so little. It is still so hard to believe I am a "Mimi" now. No matter how old you get, you will still be my babies. I love you with every beat of my heart.

A special thank you to my youngest daughter Bailey, there are no words to tell you what a special little soul you are. You have the biggest heart of anyone I know. Your unselfishness for someone so young brings me to tears. You have sacrificed a lot during your mommy writing this book. You have cheered me on always with a smile. You never complain and do so many little things just because. You have provided me with tons of hugs, tiny shoulder massages, and bought me countless cups of herbal tea. You have pitched in with everything and always tell me how proud you are of me. I am the one who is proud to be your mommy. I love you my 'Boo Bear." You sustain me and when I look in your eyes I see only the beauty in

● ●

the world. "Every time I close my eyes, I thank the Lord that I have you, and you have me too."

To my totally awesome parents Jim and Jean, it would take a few lifetimes to thank you for everything you have done for me. If my children feel about me they way I feel about you, then there could be nothing more in this world I could want. You are both the most nurturing, sacrificing, generous, loving and supportive parents anyone could ever ask for. My strength, my faith, my hope, my compassion all have been imprinted into my being because of what you have taught and shown me. I wish everyone was as lucky to be as blessed as I have been with you as my parents. You are both the sun in my world. You define all the wonderment of what a Parent and Grandparent truly is. I love you more than words can ever express.

Above all I want to give thanks to my lord and savior Jesus Christ. I have always felt your hand reaching out for me. My faith is unwavering. Through you all things are possible. You have blessed me in more ways than I could have ever hoped for.

Contents

Introduction

This is a book about the celebration of grandparenthood. Many times when we hear the delightful news that we are expectant grandparents, the first question that comes to our mind is what will my grandchildren call me? I became an expectant grandmother at the age of 41. I knew that Grandma was not a name to fit me or my personality. Grandma is a fine name and some choose that proudly, but for me it was not a good fit. In the quest for my own grandparent name, I went to the book store and looked for a book for Grandparents' names and I could not find one. I went to work in search of a perfect name to fit my personality. I asked people what their grandchildren called them. I spent hours searching the web, read magazine articles and came up with a lot of names on my own. I collected so much information that soon I had people calling me asking for my advice on a perfect name for them.

My children discussed ideas and they came up with "Mimi." I loved it. My daughter and son-in-law are deaf and Mimi was a name they could say a lot more easily than grandma.

If you are looking for a unique, easy and fun name then **The Big Book of Grandparents' Names** will become your new best friend. Whether you are looking for a specific language or want to honor your heritage or ethnic background, you are given all the information you will need to choose a perfect name for you. With over 1,000 names and 200 languages you will have plenty of choices.

● ●

Whether you would like a Native American name, a Celtic name or a fun Urban name, inside this book there is a name for you. I think it is important to honor our ethnic backgrounds. Genealogy is very popular today and I have included ethnic proverbs that perhaps you can pass down to your precious grandchildren. I have also included charts on American Sign Language and Latin Braille.

The Big Book of Grandparents' Names has up-to-date information on the new trend in unique grandparent names. I have included many resources for grandparents for the baby-boomers who are now grand-boomers. There is even a recipe for you to make with your grandchildren.

So, if you're ready to be called something other than grandmother and grandfather, you have made the first step with this book. Grab a latte, relax and have fun while you enjoy **The Big Book of Grandparents' Names**. Have a ball picking a name that's right for you.

● ●

Inspirational Quotes for Grandparents

Grandmother-Grandchild relationships are simple. Grandmas are short on criticism and long on love
~Author Unknown~

The best place to be when you're sad is on Grandpa's lap
~Author Unknown~

Grandmother- a wonderful mother with lots of practice
~Author Unknown~

It's amazing how grandparents seem so young once you become one
~Author Unknown~

Grandparents are similar to a piece of string- handy to have around and easily wrapped around the fingers of their grandchildren
~Author Unknown~

A grandmother is a mother who has a second chance
~Author Unknown~

Ethnic Proverbs for Grandparents

Perfect love sometimes does not come until the first grandchild
~Welsh Proverb~

If nothing is going well, call your grandmother
~Italian Proverb~

If you know his father and grandfather, don't worry about his son
~African Proverb~

The baby is not yet born, and yet you say that his nose is like his grandfather's
~ Indian Proverb~

You've got to do your own growing, no matter how tall your grandfather was
~Irish Proverb~

One of life's greatest mysteries is how the boy who wasn't good enough to marry your daughter can be the father of the smartest grandchild in the world
~Jewish Proverb~

The old are the precious gem in the center of the household
~Chinese Proverb~

• •

To forget one's ancestors is to be a brook without a
source, a tree without a root
~Chinese Proverb~

A people without history is like wind on the buffalo grass
~Sioux Proverb~

An ounce of blood is worth more than a pound of
friendship
~Spanish Proverb~

When you have a grandchild, you have two children
~Jewish Proverb~

Children's children are a crown to the aged, and parents
are the pride of their children
~Proverbs~

The motherless child will suckle the grandmother
~Bambara Proverb~

We are too soon old and too late wise
~Jewish Proverb~

• •

National Grandparents Day

National Gandparents Day is the 1st Sunday after Labor Day

Marian McQuade, founded Grandparents Day in 1973 in West Virginia. McQuade was a homemaker and a mother of 15 children. She spent 5 more years bringing all of the U.S. States on board and now Grandparents Day is a U.S. Holiday.

In 1978, five years after its West Virginia inception, the United States Congress passed legislation proclaiming the first Sunday after Labor Day as National Grandparents Day, an annual celebration to honor grandparents and recognize their contributions to society and the link they provide younger generations to America's national heritage and traditions. The proclamation was signed by President Jimmy Carter on September 6, 1979.

Proclamation 4679- National Grandparents Day- September 6, 1979
By the President of the United States of America, Jimmy Carter

Grandparents Day Proclamation

As we seek to strengthen the enduring values of the family, it is appropriate that we honor our grandparents.

September was chosen for the holiday, to signify the "autumn years" of life.

Today this event, begun by only a few, is observed by millions throughout the United States.

● ●

Official Flower of Grandparents Day

The official flower of Grandparents day is the Forget-me-Not. The Forget-Me-Not was adopted as the official flower for Grandparents Day by the National Grandparents Day Council on April 2, 1999. The choice of the Forget-Me-Not serves not only as encouragement to create lasting memories by nurturing relationships between generations, but also as a poignant reminder that the time to pursue those relationships is limited.

Official Song of Grandparents Day

The official song for Grandparents Day is "A Song for Grandma and Grandpa," by Johnny Prill. Prill's songs have been performed or recorded by music legends Bobby Vinton, Wayne Newton, among others.

● ●

Grandparents Dump Cake

20 ounce can crushed pineapple undrained
21 ounce can cherry pie filling
1 box yellow cake mix
2 sticks butter each cut into 12 slices
1/4 cup chopped pecans

Preheat oven to 350.

Spray rectangular baking pan with cooking spray. Dump undrained pineapple into pan and spread out evenly. Spread cherry pie filling evenly on top of the pineapple. Sprinkle cake mix evenly over the cherry and pineapple layers. Cut butter into slices with a butter knife and place slices evenly over cake mix. Sprinkle nuts on top. Place in oven and bake for 1 hour.

Serve warm or at room temperature.

Great names for GRANDMOTHERS

....

Aaaga

Aaga

Aaji

Aaka

Aana

Aanaga

Aanak

Aanaruaba

Aanatsiaq

Abba

Abi

Abooto

Abuela

Abuelita

Abui

Aeea

Aiti

Ajibai

Ajja

....

• •

Ajji
Ala
Alto
Ama sani
Amatci
Ambuya koz
Ami
Amm umma
Amma
Ammamma
Ammi
Ammo
Anneanne
Anvamm
Anya
Anyóka
Apachi
Aphyi
Apple-pie
Apples
Aryia
Astina mere
Ava
Ave
Avia

• •

Avino
Avo
Avoa
Awila
Ayamm
Ayaya
Ayeeyo

B

Bá
Ba ba
Baaba
Baba
Baba baka
Babaanne
Babaiyaa
Babci
Babcia
Babchi
Babi
Babic'ka
Babicka
Babka

Babo
Babsie
Babushka
Babusia
Baby
Badda
Bagoo
Baka baba
Baka
Balluck
Bam bam
Bam maw
Bamba
Bamma
Bana
Banana
Banma
Beautiful
Be ma
Beam ma
Beamer
Bebia
Bebop
Bedstemoder
Beebaw
Beerma

Great Names for Grandmothers

Bella
Beppe
Bestemamma
Bestemor
Bibi
Big gram
Big grandma
Big mama
Bingo
Binky
Birdie
Bobaloo
Bobo
Bomma
Bonbon
Booma
Boomer
Bootie
Boowa
Bopchi
Boppy
Bubbie
Bubbles
Bubbly
Bube
Bubeeh

Bubu yalewa
Buby
Budna
Budsi
Buella
Bum
Bum bum
Bumpy
Bunia
Bunica
Bunicut
Bunny
Busia
Butchy
Buyuk-anne

C

Caccara
Cakie
Calufuru
Ce Ce
Cha cha
Cheer ma
Cheetah

Cherry
Chickie
Choo
Chuckles
Cici
Coco
Cocoa
Cookie
Cracker
Ctapy
Cuckoo
Cupcake

D

Daadi
Dadi
Dadong
Dainty
Daisy
Damma
Dancer
Dancey
Dandy

Danna
Darling
Dear
Debma
Deda
Deeda
Dee Dee
Dida
Didi
Diddie
Didima
Dimples
Diva
Divina
Divinity
Doda
Dodie
Doggy boo boo
Dolly
Dowager
Drama
Dreamer
Dream Nana
Dreamy
Duckie
Ducky
Dyido

E

Eana-nana
Eemah
Eestaw-Ista
Elisi
Elsi
E-Ma
Emaw
Emma
Emmaw
Ene
Enisi
Essie
Etah

F

Fafa
Fairy Grandma
Fairy Grandmother
Fancy
Fea
Fi Fi

Fluff
Fluffy
Foxy
Frannie
Fringe
Fu Fu

G

G ma
G mom
Ga
Gabbe
Gabby
Gaga
Gaggy
Gam
Gammie
Gankie
Gann
Gannie
Ganny
Garva
Gee
Geemaw

Great Names for Grandmothers

• •

Ge-Ge
Ghee
Gibba
Gibbie
Gido
Giggi
Giggles
Giggly
Giggy
Gigi
Gigia
Gimmie
Ging
Ginga
Ginger
Gisela
Gjyshe
Glama
Glamma
Glo Glo
Go Go Grama
Goggie
Goggy
Go-Go
Gom
Gommie

• •

Gommy
Gonga
Grady
Graga
Gram
Grama
Grambo
Gramiar
Gramle
Gramma
Gramma great
Grammah
Grammbo
Grammie
Grammlemor
Grammommie
Grammy
Grams
Gramsy
Gran
Gran gran
Grana
Grancy
Grand meow
Grand mimi
Grandam

Great Names for Grandmothers

• •

Grandberry
Grandee
Grandismo
Grandma
Grandma goose
Grandma in law
Grand-maman
Grandmamma
Grand-mere
Grandmerry
Grandmom
Grandmommy
Grandmoms
Grandmoo
Grandmother
Grandmother Goose
Grandmotherly
Grandmuffin
Grandmums
Grandmutter
Grandnan
Grandness
Grandy
Granite
Gran'ma
Granmomma

• •

Granna

Grannie

Granno

Granny

Grannymama

Granola

Grantique

Gray-gray

Great gran

Great grandmother

Great mother

Great nanny

Grebby

Greena Grootmoeder

Granmatre

Groovy

Grossmutter

Grum

Grummy

Gumby

Gummy

Gwanma

H

Hain hain
Halmeoni
Halmoki
Hana
Hapa
Happy
Hausis
Hausisse
Henna
Henvamm
Honey
Honeybee
Honey-buns
Honeylove
Hope
Hoppie
Hot glama
Hot grama
Huggy
Hun Hun

I

Iaia
Impo lelang
Impo
Ina ferik
Ina
Inan-bei
Ingkong
Isoáiti
Iu-naoy

J

Jadda
Jaja
Jamie
Jamma
Jammie
Jaryi
Jedda
Jeeda
Jidda

Jidon
Jimmies
Jjajja
Jojo

K

Kaki
Kakie
Kami
Kay wayboro
Kia
Kiki
Kinky
Kishka
Koko
Koko ya mwasi
Koko ya-ke:nto
Kuabi
Kuia
Kukax
Kuku
Kukun
Kupuna

Kupuna ka-ne
Kupuna wahine

L

Lala
Lalu
Lana
Lassie
Lela
Little mama
Lola
Loli
Loli and Pop - Grandparent's
Lolipop
Lolly
Lolly pops
Looloo
Love love
Lovely
Lovie

M

Ma

Ma tare

Ma tiara

Maa

Maadar-e bozorg

Maataamahili

Mackey

Madar bozorg

Madear

Madiar

Madonnava

Mae mae

Maga

Mager

Magga

Mai mai

Maime

Maimeo

Mairm

Mairma

Majika stará

Majika

Mam lo

Mam wow
Mama
Mama2
Mamabear
Mamaie
Mamalee
Maman
Mamas an
Mamaw
Mambo
Mame
Mamey
Mam-gu
Mami tumbuna
Mamie
Mami-sani
Mammal
Mamm-baour
Mamm-gozh
Mammi
Mammo
Mammothrept
Mammow
Mammy
Mamomy
Mampsie

Great Names for Grandmothers

Mams
Mamsita
Mamy
Mannedda
Mardi
Mardo
Marmalade
Marmalee
Marme
Marmee
Marmi
Marmie
Marnie
Mashie
Mater
Mathair chriona
Mauka
Maw-maw
Maynah
Mee maw
Meemer
Meemoss
Meemuh
Mee-thao
Meimie
Meitheir mhor

Mema
Meme
Memere
Memerr
Memo
Memog
Memom
Me-mom
Memot
Memuzzer
Mere
Mere mere
Metzmayr
Mica
Mil
Milky
Millie
Mim
Mima
Mimaw
Mime
Mimi
Minana
Minmaw
Minnow
Mmakhulu

Great Names for Grandmothers

Mmemogolo

Mocha

Mociute

Moggie

Moggy

Mom Grandma

Mom Granna

Moma

Momaw

Mombo

Momeo

Momette

Momma mia

Mommasita

Mommita

Mommom

Mom-mom

Mommone

Mommy Grandma

Momo

Momon

MomsieMonee

Money

Moo moo

Moogy

Moonbeam

Moonie
Mop
Mops
Morai
More mommy
Mormor
Mor-mor
Mormor
Mou lou
Mu qin
Muddy
Mudgy
Muffer
Muffin
Muggy
Mum
Muma
Mumme
Mummers
Mummica
Mummo
Mummu
Mummy
Mumpsy
Mumsie

• •

Muna
Munny
Murmur
Muthassi
Muttie
Muv
Muzzie
Mwarree
My my
My nanner
Mymomma

N

Na nah
Naana
Nagyanya
Nahuatl
Nai nai
Nain
Nai-nai
Nam
Namaw

• •

Nami
Namma
Nammy
Namo
Namshim
Nana
Nana love
Nana nena
Nana puddin
Nanagrandma
Nanamamma
Nanamy
Nandy
Nani
Nani dadu
Nanma
Nan-ma
Nanna
Nan-nan
Nanni
Nannuk
Nanny
Nanoo
Nanzie
Nauna
Naunee

Great Names for Grandmothers

Ne Ne
Nee nee
Neema
Neenamaa
Neeny
Nema
Nene
Nenek
Nenibe
Ni ni
Ninama
Ning
Nini
Ninna
Ninny
Niyang
Nne-m
No no
Nokomis
Non nee
Nona
Nonna
Nonnie
Nonno
Nonny
Nookomis

Norni
Nu nu
Nun nun
Nuna
Nunong babae
Nyanya
Nyogokuru

O

Oba-cha
Oba-chan
Oggy
Oh my
Old ma
Oma
Omi
Ommie
Ota
Ouma

P

Paati-tamil
Pagiging lola
Pawsie
Payako
Peaches
Pepin
Pepper
Peppy
Pinky
Pitty pat
Playma
Play-play
Popo
Predchodkyna
Pretty
Princess
Prissy
Puddy
Predchodkyna

Q

Queenie

S

Safta
Sani
Sasa
Savta
Seanathair
Seanmhair
Seanmhathair
Senele
Seno-mater
Set ayat
Shenn shenn warree
Shenn voir
Shenn waree
Shimasani
Shinasani
Silly
Sittu

Skippy
Slo-ma
Slomom
Snuggles
Softee
Sparkly
Sprinkles
Squeaky
Stará mama
Stáry otec
Stumpy
Sugar
Sugar smacks
Sunny
Supergran
Sweetie
Sweetums

T

Tae-tae
Taita
Tat tatik
Tatta

Te ta
Te vama-te
Teensy
Teeny
Teeta
Teetay
Teta
Tetah
Thakurma
Thakur-ma
Tina o matua
Tinkerbell
Tita
Titi
Tuin
Turtle
Tut-wahini
Tweety
Twink
Twinkie
Twinkles
Two mama

U

Uaci
Ubabemkhula
Uelita
Ugogo
U-ku-wahine puna
Umakhula
Umakhulu
Umm
Unci

V

Vanaema
Vecmate
Vovo
Vye moman

W

Wela
White nanna
Wiper

Y

Yaa
Yaay
Yane
Yaya
Ya-ya
Yee yee
Yi Yi
Yia yia
Yucca
Yums

Z

Zinha

Great names for
GRANDFATHERS

A woowe
A yayu
Aata
Abdu
Abkoow
Abu
Abuelito
Abuelo
Achachi
Adax
Aito
Aitona
Aja
Ajja
Ajoba
Alaala
Alo
Aman tuan
Aman-tuak

• •

Amyia
Anguula
Apo
Apóka
Appollo
Appooppan
Ari
Ata
Ataata
Ataataga
Ataatatsiaq
Athair crionna
Athair mor
Avi
Avo
Avó
Avô
Avohana
Avus
Awow

• •

B

Baba
Baba gjysh
Baba
Bababubs
Babbobe
Babo
Babua
Badda
Bald gramps
Bampa
Bampsie
Bampy
Banpa
Bapér
Bawegewre
Bear
Bedebpir
Bepa
Bepaw
Bestefader
Bestefar
Bestepappa
Big boss

Big daddy

Big gramps

Big grandpa

Big papu

Big pop

Big poppa

Blah blah

Bo bo

Bomp

Bompa

Bompy

Bonpa

Boober

Booboo

Bookdaddy

Boomer

Boompa–Phew

Booper

Booute

Bop-bee

Boppa

Boppie

Boppy

Bubba

Buddy

Buello

Bul bul
Bully
Bumbpa
Bumie
Bumpa
Bumps
Bunic
Bunicut
Butch
Buva
Buyuk baba

C

Cacaru
Calafuru
Campa
Cap
Cappy
Caps
Captain
Captain grumps
Checkers
Chief
Chip

Chippy
Chirpy
Choppers
Chuchu
Colli
Cree

D

Da
Da pa
Daada
Daadi
Dada
Dadamoshai
Daddio
Daddor
Daddy O
Dadju
Dadu
Dadushka
Dady nana
Daideo

Dappy
Dar
DD
Dé
Ddedecek
Deda
Dedaw
Dede
Dedecek
Dedko
Dedo
Dedushka
Deka
Diado
Didi
Didler
Divo
Djed
Djeda
Djedo
Dodo
Doodad
Drampa
Dub
Dubba

Duck-duck
Dude
Dude dad
Duke
Dumpa
Dyido
Dzia diza
Dziadek
Dziadzio

E

E du da
E dudi
Edudi
Eepah
Eitheir mor
Eka djed

F

Faé
Faeder

• •

Fafie
Famor
Farfar
Farnarner
Fast-pop
Fat pap
Fatpapa
Fatpop
Fatpoppa
Fil
Fish
Fuqin

G

G bear
G pop
Gada
Gaka
Gammlefar
Gamps
Gankie
G-daddy
Gdaddyo

• •

G-did
Geebear
Geepaw
Giggles
Giggly
Gigi
Ging ging
Gingo
Gjysh
Go go
Go-daddy
Gogi
Gong
Gongo
Gop
G-pa
Grady
Gram
Grammlefa
Gramoster
Gramp
Grampa
Grampabear
Grampkapop
Gramps

Great Names for Grandfathers

Grampy
Grampybear
Grand D
Grand dad
Grand Di
Grand farter
Grand Marne
Grand pa pa
Grand papa
Grand pupon
Granda
Grandad
Grandan
Grandboss
Grandbubba
Granddaddy
Grand-dude
Grandee
Grandesagung
Grandfather
Grandfather bear
Grandio
Grandmeir
Grandnard
Grando

Grandpa
Grandpa buttons
Grandpa foo
Grandpa snuggles
Grandpadaddy
Grandpam
Grandpap
Grandpapa
Grandpa-pop
Grandpappy
Grand-pere
Grandpop
Grandpoppa
Grandpops
Grandpup
Grandsire
Grandslam
Grandude
Grandy
Granga
Granin
Granlin
Granola
Granpa
Granpatre
Granpee

Great Names for Grandfathers

Granpie
Granpo
Granpop
Grandpoppa
Grandpops
Grandpup
Grandsire
Grandslam
Grandude
Grandy
Granga
Granin
Granlin
Granola
Granpa
Granpatre
Granpee
Granpie
Granpo
Granpop
Gran'puh
Graydar
Graypa
Graypop
Great pa
Grenbaja

Gringo
Groan
Grootvader
Grossdaddy
Grossvater
Grum
Grummy
Grump
Grumpa
Grumpo
Grumps
Grumpy
Gruncle
Grundie
Guapo
Guedo
Gum
Gumby
Gummiebear
Gummy
Gums
Guppa
Guppy
Gups
Gwanpa

H

Halabeoji
Halaboji
Harabujee
Hendas
Hoho
Hoppa
Hsotha
Huggybear

I

Iaio
Ingkong
Isoisa

J

Jadd
Jaddee

Jaja
Jaja
Jatun yaya
Jazz
Jazzie
Jebbie
Jeddo
Jid
Jidi
Jido
Jidu
Jiichan
Jishag mooar
Jishag
Jjajja

K

Kakek
Kaklang
Ka-ne
Kayalboro
Kokato
Koko ya bakala

Koko ya mobali
Ku-ku
Ku-ku-
Kumpie
Kupuna

L

Latuk

Lefty

Lelang
Lelong
Lokoko
Lol
Loli and Pop -Grandparent's
Lolo

M

Maataamaha
Mack
Mack daddy
Mack daddyo

Big Book of Grandparents' Names

Mackerel

Mackey

Mackie

Mam

Maneddu

Mate

Manny

Mano

Meeoss

Memo

Metzhayr

Mickey

Mishomis

Missiavu

Mmakhulu

Modor

Morai

More

Morfar

Mornie

Mor-phar

Mumpa

Musher

Mypoppa

Mzee

N

Naana
Nabba
Nagyapa
Namshim
Nannu
Nanny
Needaddy
Neemo
Neenadaa
Nene
Ngamuri
Nightnight
Nine
Nixkamichi
Nna m-
Nokomis
Non
Nonno
Nonny
Nono
Noodle
Npaarao

Ntatemogolo
Nunong lalaki

O

Ojichan
Oji-chan
Ojiisan
Old gramps
Oldie
Oldpa
Ole dodo
Omatuatama
Omi
Ôna
Opa
Opaatje
Opa-dyado
Opis
Ota
Oupa

P

Pa minnow

Pa pas an

Pabby

Pabrown

Packal

Padrina

Paka

Pake

Pal

Palo

Palsie

Palsy

Palz

Pami

Pamp

Pampo

Pamps

Panii-sani

Paoo

Pap U

Papa2

Papa

Papa bear
Papa bill
Papa boy
Papa daddy
Papa Doc
Papagrande
Papalee
Papa monster
Papando
Papasito
Papa papa
Papa tumbuna
Papaw
Papaya
Papere
Papeta
Papi
Paplito
Papo
Papoose
Papoppy
Pappa
Pappap
Pappie

Pappoo
Pappous
Papps
Pappy
Paps
Papsito
Papu
Pargan
Pater
Paw
Paw paw
Pawpee
Pawsey
Paw-thoo
Pedar bozorg
Pedar-e-bozorg
Peepaw
Peepuh
Pepa
Pepe
Pepere
Pepop
Pepper
Petah
Pez

Phar-phar
Pinto
Pipa
Pipes
Pippie
Pippy
Piruk
Playpa
Pompa
Poo bear
Poopie
Poopoo
Pop
Pop grandpa
Pop pop
Pop u lar
Pop up
Popcorn
Poposito
Poppa
Poppa G
Poppa GP
Poppair
Popper
Poppers

Poppie
Poppies
Poppop
Poppops
Poppy
Poppy2
Poppyseed
Poprocket
Poprocks
Pops
Popsicle
Popsie
Popsito
Popzie
Pramatamaha
Predchodca
Pyjaw

R

Raibe
Rooster

S

Saba
Safta
Sawa
Scratchy
Scruffy
Seanair
Seanathair
Seedo
Sekuru kko mz
Seneli
Senelis
Seno-tato
Shenayr
Sheriff
Shimasani
Si je kenek
Silly grandpa
Slo pa
Slo pop
Sogokuru
Sparky
Spicy
Spike

Squinty
Squirt
Stari oee
Stubby
Sugar pappy

T

Ta Da
Ta- grandpa
Taatax
Tatta
Taattaa
Tad-paour
Taid
Taitaguasu
Tamazight
Tan-wela
Tas-gwynn
Tat
Tata
Tataie
Tato
Tat'omkhulu

Tattoo
Tb-Kd
Thakurda
Thakurdada
Thakur-dada
Thakur-da-o
Thar poo dta
Tito
Tjamu
Togbui
Toot
Tootsie
Toughpop
Truckie pa
Tsoyeee
Tuakaabida
Tunkaschila
Tupuna wahine
Tutu
Tu-tu
Twopapa

U

Uakaana
Ubabamkhula
Ugogo
Ukki
Uleito
Uwgun aab

V

Vaari
Vanaisa
Vater
Vecais tev
Vecte-vs
Von
Vovo
Vye popa

W

Wai gong
Wappa
Whiskers
White grampa
Wicky
Wish pa

Y

Yayo
Ye ye
Yeh-yeh
Yi-ey

Z

Zaide
Zayde
Zeidy
Zeydeh

Languages Around The World

Language/ No. Speakers	Region	Grandmother	Grandfather
Abkhaz 95,000	Abkhazia	Babo	Abdu
Aboriginal 400	Australia	Nannuk Kukun	Ngamuri
Afrikaans 6,000,000	South Africa	Ouma	Oupa
Albanian 5,000,000	Albania	Gjyshe	Baba Gjysh
Amharic 14,000,000	Ethiopia	Set Ayat	Gjysh
Arabic 165,000,000	Algeria Egypt Iraq Jordan Kuwait Lebanon Libya Mauritania Morocco Saudi Arabia Somalia Sudan Syria Yemen	Jeeda Tae-Tae Jidda Umm Taita	Jaddee Jadd Guedo Jed Abu
Aramaic 445,000	Turkey Syria	Sittu	Sawa

Big Book of Grandparents' Names

Language/ No. Speakers	Region	Grandmother	Grandfather
Aramaic Is Believed To Have Been The Mother Tongue Of Jesus	Iraq Iran Azerbaijan Lebanon		
Armenian 2,000,000	Armenia Iran	Metzmayr Tat Tatik	Metzhayr Papik, Hav
Assamese 12,000,000	India	Tu:N	Kokato
Austrian 102,000,000	Austria	Mashie	Vater
Australian 300,000	Australia	Nana	Poppy
Aymara 2,000,000	Bolivia Peru	Apachi	Achachi
Azeri 14,000,000	Iran Azerbaijan	Ne Ne	Baba
Balinese 3,000,000	Indonesia	Dadong	Kakiang
Baluchi 4,000,000	Pakistan Iran Afghanistan	Balluck	Piruk
Bantu 4,407,000	Bostwana Tswana	Nyogokuru	Sogokuru

Languages Around The World

Language/ No. Speakers	Region	Grandmother	Grandfather
Basque 660,000	NE Spain SW France	Amatchi	Aitona
Batak 3,500,000	Indonesia	Niyang	Kumpie
Belorussian 7,500,000	Belarus	Ctapyxa	Dziadek
Bengali 180,000,000	Bangladesh India	Didi Dida Hana	Dadamoshai Thakurdada Pramatam-Aha
Berber 12,000,000	Morocco Tamazight Algeria	Jedda Henna	Jaddee
Bosnian 100,000	Bosnia	Baka Nana Majka Baba Nena	Eka Dedo Majka Stara Djed Deda
Bulgarian 8,500,000	Bulgari Belgium Moldovia	Oma Diado Baba	Opa Npaarao Dyado
Burmese 21,000,000	Burma	Tbgm	Tbkd
Brazilian 196,000,000	Brazil	VÔvo	VovÔ
Calabrese 2,000,000	Italy	Nanna	Nannu

Big Book of Grandparents' Names

Language/ No. Speakers	Region	Grandmother	Grandfather
Cantonese 64,000,00	Hong Kong	Maa Gung Mou Lou	Gong
Catalan 6,500,000	Spain	Àvia Ava Laia	Avi Padrina Laio
Catanese 4,500,000	Italy	Nanna	Nannu
Cham 230,000	Cambodia Vietnam	Payako	Lokoko
Chechen 900,000	Russia	Neenamaa	Neenadaa
Chinese 1,125,000,000	China Taiwan Hong Kong Malaysia Singapore	Ma Mu Qin Ba Ba	Fu Qin Wai Gong Ye Ye
Corsican 127,000	Corsica	Mammone Caccara Minana	Babbobe Cacaru Missiavu
Creole 375,000,000	Haiti	Memerr	Papere
Crioulo 750,000	Guine Senegal Cape Verde Islands	Mami Tumbuna	Papa Tumbuna
Croatian 100,000	Croatia	Baba, Baka	Djed,Djeda

Languages Around The World

Language/ No. Speakers	Region	Grandmother	Grandfather
Czech 12,000,000	Czeck Republic	Babic'ka Babicka	Dedecek De'ddedecek
Danish 5,500,000	Denmark	Bedstemoder	Bestefader
Dominican 9,500,000	Dominican Republic	Guela	Guelo
Dutch 20,000,000	Netherlands Amsterdam	Grootmoeder Bomma Oma	Grootvader Opa Bompa Opaatje
English 375,000,000	Australia Canada India Ireland Malaysia Singapore South Africa Sri Lanka United Kingdom United Sates Of America	Grandmother Grandma Grandmom Grandmommy Gram Grams Granny	Grandfather Grandpa Grandad Granddaddy Gramp Gramps Grampy
Esperanto 100,000	France	Avino	Avohana
Estonian 1,100,000	Estonia	Vanaema	Vanaisa
Ewe- Fon 4,000,000	Togo Benin	Mama	Togbui
Farsi 40,000,000	Iraq	Maadar-E Bozorg	Pedar-E Bozorg

87

Big Book of Grandparents' Names

Language/ No. Speakers	Region	Grandmother	Grandfather
Fataluku 30,000	New Guinea	Calu furu	Cala furu
Fijian 350,000	Fiji	Bubu Yalewa	Tutu
Filipino 90,000,000	Philipines	Nunong-Babae Impo Lelang Pagiging Lola	Nunong Lalaki Ingkong-Lelong Lolo, Apo
Finnish 5,000,000	Finland Sweden Russia	Isoäiti Mummo Mummu	Isoisä Vaari Ukki Pappa
Flemish 20,000,000	Dutch	Bomma	Bonpa
French 70,000,000	France Canada Belgium	Grand-Maman Gramiar Memere Mamy	Grand-Pere Grand Papa Poppair Pepere Papy
Frisian 700,000	Netherlands	Baaba	Pake
Friulian 794,000	Italy	Ave	Von
Galician 3,000,000	Spain	Avoa	Avó
Georgian 3,900,000	Georgia	Bebia,Babo	Babua,Papa

Languages Around The World

● ●

Language/ No. Speakers	Region	Grandmother	Grandfather
German 120,000,000	Germany Austria Russia Switzerland Fazakhstan Romania	Oma Grossmutter	Opa
Greek 11,500,000	Greece Cyprus	Yaya, Nona Mammi Yia Yia	Pappous Papou, Papu
Guarani 7,000,000	Paraguay Argentina	Jaryi	Taitaguasu
Hawaiian 2,000	Hawaii	Tutu U-Ku-Wahine- Puna	Ku-Ku- Ku-Ku-Ka-Ne
Hebrew 3,000,000	Israel	Savta	Saba
Hungarian 15,000,000	Hungary Romania	Anyóka Nagyanya	Apóka Nagyapa
Icelandic 250,000	Iceland	Amma	Afi
Igbo 12,000,000	Nigeria	Nne-M	Nna M-
India Bengali 180,000	Bengladesh	Didal Paati-Tami Nani Thakur-Ma	Thakur-Da O Dadu Thakur-Dada
India Gujarati 60,000,000	Gujarat	Amma	Baaba

● ●

Big Book of Grandparents' Names

Language/ No. Speakers	Region	Grandmother	Grandfather
India Telugu 66,000,000	N. Sri Lanka	Ammamma Nanamamma	Dadu,Nana Tata
India Urdu 100,000,000	Pakistan	Nanni Naana	Daadi Daada
Indonesian 23,000,000	Indonesia	Nenek Eyang	Kakek
Israelie 7,000,000	Israel	Safta	Zeydeh
Interlingua 1,000	Scandinavia	Granmatre	Granpatre
Irish 538,000	Ireland	Máthair-Chríona	Athair-Críonna
Italian 60,000,000	Italy	Nonna	Nonno
Japenese 120,000,000	Japan	Oba-Chan	Oji-Chan Jiichan
Judeo 200,000	Portugese	Nona	Nono
Khmer 8,000,000	Cambodia	Jidon	Yi-Ey
Korean 63,000,000	Korea	Halmeoni	Halabeoji
Kriol 10,000	Australia	Greni	Grenbaja

Languages Around The World

Language/ No. Speakers	Region	Grandmother	Grandfather
Kru 2,2000,000	Liberia Sierra Leone	Harabujee	Koro
Kurdish 20,000,000	Iraq Turkey Syria	Anneanne Bedebpir	Bawegewre Bapêr
Kuwait 165,000,000	Lebanon Libya Mauritania Morrocco Saudi Arabia Somalia Sudan Syria Yemen	Jadda, Umm Tae-Tae	Jadd,Abu Guedo
Lao 15,000,000	Laos Lanna Thailand	Mee-Thao	Paw-Thoo
Latin 1,000,000,000	Rome	Avia	Avus
Latvian 1,500,000	Latvia	Vecmate Opis Te Vama-Te TevTeVama-Te	Vecais Vecte-Vs
Lingala 2,000,000	Congo	Koko YaMwasi	Koko YaMobal
Lithuanian 3,500,000	Lithuania	Senele Mociute	Senelis' Bobute
Luganda 3,000,000	S. Uganda	Jjajja	Jjajja

Big Book of Grandparents' Names

Language/ No. Speakers	Region	Grandmother	Grandfather
Macedonian 2,250,000	Macedonia	Baba	Dedo
Malagasy 10,000,000	Madagascar	Nenibe	Raibe
Malay 35,000,000	Malaysia	Nenek	Kakek
Malayalam 22,000,000	India	Muthassi Amm Umma	Muthachnan Appooppan
Maltese 350,000	Malta	Nanna	Nannu
Maori 500,000	New Zealand	Kuia	Tupuna-Wahine
Mandarin 885,000,000	China	Nai-Nai	Yeh-Yeh
Nepali 11,000,000	Nepal	Wela	Tan-Wela
Norweigan 5,000,000	Norway	Gammlemor Bestemor	Gammlefa Bestefar
Occitan 3,000,000	France	Pepin	Papeta
Palestinian 10,570,000	Palestine	Teetay, Teeta	Seedo, Jeedo
Pitjantjatjara 4,000	Aboriginese	Kami	Tjamu

Languages Around The World

Language/ No. Speakers	Region	Grandmother	Grandfather
Punjabi 60,000,000	Pakistan	Nani	Daada
Persian 31,000,000	Afghanistan	Madar Bozorg	Pedar Bozorg
Polish 40,000,000	Poland	Busia, Babcia	Dzia Dzia
Puerto Rican 39,000,000	Puerto Rico	Grandismo Babci	Grandesa Jaja
Portuguese 155,000,000	Portugal Brazil	Vovo, Avo Zinha	Avó Avô
Quebecois 7,000	Canada	Meme	Pepe
Quechua 10,400,000	South America	Awila	Jatun Yaya
Romagnolo 2,000,000	Italy	Nuna	Non
Romani 3,000,000	Roma	Mamaie	Tataie
Romanian 24,000,000	Romania	Bunica	Bunic Dadushka
Romansch 65,000	Switzerland	Tatta	Tat
Russian 175,000,000	Russia	Babushka	Dedushka Dadushka

Big Book of Grandparents' Names

Language/ No. Speakers	Region	Grandmother	Grandfather
Rwanda 12,000,000	Uganda	Nyogokuru	Sogokuru
Samoan 200,000	Hawaii	Tina OMatua	OMatua Tama
Sanskrit 435	Greater India	Maataamahii	Maata-amaha
Santali 6,000	Bangladesh	Aaji	Aja
Sardinian 16,000,000	Italy	Ayaya Mannedda	A Yayu Maneddu
Scottish 4,400,400	Scotland	Seanmhair	Nonnu
Serbian 18,500,000	Serbia	Baba, Nana Baba Baka	Deda, Djed Deka
Sinhalese 19,000,000	Sri Lanka	Ommie	Si Je Kenek
Slovak 5,500,000	Slovakia	Babicka Starý Otec Predchodkyna	Dedko Predchodca
Slovenian 2,000,000	Slovenia	Stará Mama	Stari Oee
Somalia 95,000,000	Somali	Abooto Macooyo Ayeeyo	Abkoow A Woowe Awow
Sotho 4,300,000	South African	Ugogo	Ubabam-khula

Languages Around The World

Language/ No. Speakers	Region	Grandmother	Grandfather
South American 382,000,000	South America	Ajji	Naana
Spanish 225,000,000	Chile Bolivia Cuban	Abuela Abuelita Tita Ala	Abuelito Abuelo Tito Alo
Swahili 400,000,000	Kenya	Nyanya	Mzee
Swazi 1,600,000	Mozambique	Ubabemkhula	Ugogo
Swedish 9,000,000	Sweden Finland	Mormor	Morfar Farfar
Syrian 19,000,000	Arabic	Teta	Jidu
Tagalog 22,000,000	Philippines	Impo	Ingkong
Tahitian 100,000	French Polynesia	Ingkong	Lelang
Tamil 68,000,000	Sri lanka	Ayamma	T atta
Telugu 45,000,000	India	Iu-Naoy	Taattaa
Tetun 800,000,000	S.E. Asia	Inan-Bei Ina Ferik	Aman-Tuak Aman Tuan

Big Book of Grandparents' Names

Language/ No. Speakers	Region	Grandmother	Grandfather
Thai 60,000,000	Thailand	Yaay Yaa	Thar Poo Dta
Tup'namba 400	Brazil	Aryia	Amyia
Turkish 50,000,000	Turkey	Anneanne Babaanne	Dede,Nene Buyukbaba
Turkmen 4,000,000	Afghanistan	Ene	Baba
Ukranian 45,000,000	Ukraine	Babusia, Baba	Dyido
Urdu 60,000,000	Pakistan	Daadi	Daadaa
Uzbek 16,000,000	Afghanistan	Bibi Doda	BoboBuva
Valencian 9,100,000	Spain	Yaya	Yayo
Venda 87,000	South Africa	Mmakhulu	Mmakhulu
Venetian 2,000,000	Italy	Nona	Nono
Vietnamese 55,000,000	Vietnam	Bà	Ông
West Frisian 360,000	Netherlands	Beppe	Pake

Languages Around The World

Language/ No. Speakers	Region	Grandmother	Grandfather
Xhosa 7,900,000	South Africa	Umakhulu	Tat'omkhulu
Yiddish 2,000,000	Israel Russia Ukraine United States of America	Baba Iya	Zaide,Zeydeh
Yugoslavian 23,724,000	Yugoslavia Kosovo	Baka Baba	Jidi,Jido Jid
Zapotec 500,000	Mexico	Abuela	Anguula
Zarma 2,200,000	S.W. Nigeria	Kay Wayboro	Kay Alboro
Zeneize 61,000,000	Genoa-Italy	Madonnava	Papagrande
Zulu 450,000	South Africa	Umakhulua	Ubabam-khula

Eskimo Languages

Language/ No. Speakers	Region	Grandmother	Grandfather
Aluet 460	Alaska	Kukax	Adax,Taatax
Alutig 400	Alaska	Aanaga	Ata
Inuit 85,000	Canada	Aanak	Latuk

Big Book of Grandparents' Names

• •

Language/ No. Speakers	Region	Grandmother	Grandfather
Inupiaq 3,500	N. Alaska	Aanaga	Ataataga
Inuktitut 30,000	E. Canada	Aanaruaba	Ataatatsiaq
Kalaallisut 47,000	Greenland	Aaka	Alaala
Naukanski 70	Siberia	Aanatsiaq	Ataata
Yuit 1,400	C. Siberia	Aaga	Ata
Yup'ik 10,000	Alaska, Usa	Aana	Aata

**Native
American
Languages**

Algonquin 130,000,000	Wyoming	Hausis,Hausisse	Nixkamich
Apachean 9,000	Arizona	Choo	-Tsoyee
Aztec 1,045,000	Mexico	Nahuatl	Colli
Cherokee 10,000	Appalachians	Enisi	E Du Da
Cheyenne 1,721	Oklahoma Montana	Namshim Nokomis	Nokomis Namshim

• •

Languages Around The World

Language/ No. Speakers	Region	Grandmother	Grandfather
Dakota 26,000	Missouri	Uaci Kuabi	Tuakaabida Uakaana
Lakota 754	North Dakota	Unci	Tunkaschila
Mohawk 3,000	Canada New York	Eestaw-Ista	Hsotha
Navajo 178,000	Utah	Ama Sani	Shimasani
Ojibwe 80,000	Canada	Nookomis	Mishomis
Sioux 26,000	Nebraska	Ina	Tunkashila

Insular Celtic Language

Goidelic:

Language/ No. Speakers	Region	Grandmother	Grandfather
Irish 80,000	Ireland	Seanathair	Seanathair
Manx 1,600	Wales	Mwarree Shenn Voir	Jishag Mooar Shenayr
Scots Gaelic 58,000	Scotland	Seanmhair Seno-Mater	Seanair Seno-Tato
Mixed-Shelta 86,000	Ireland	Karb	Kriš-Gater

Big Book of Grandparents' Names

Language/ No. Speakers	Region	Grandmother	Grandfather
Brythonic:			
Breton 500,000	NW France	Mamm-Baour	Tad-Paour
Cornish 519,400	Cornwall	Anvamm Henvamm	Sira Wynn Tas-Gwynn
Welsh 500,000	Wales	Mam-Gu Nain	Tad-Cu Taid
Urban: Fun Languages			
Cajun 3,500	Louisiana	Vye Popa	Vye Moman
Chicano Unknown	New Mexico	Tesquela	Paruno
Da Kine 600,000	Hawaii	Kupunawahine	Kupunakane
Ebonics Unknown	Lousiana	Grandmoms	Grandpops
Elven Unknown	N. Europe	I,Osi I,Osu	U,Osi U,Osu
Gullah 250,000	South Carolina	Gran'maamy	Gran'puh
Spanglish Unknown	New Mexico	Guela	Guelo
Tex Mex Unknown	Texas	Abuela	Abuelo

• •

American Sign Language

To fingerspell Grandmother and Grandfather, spell out the letters in the chart below.

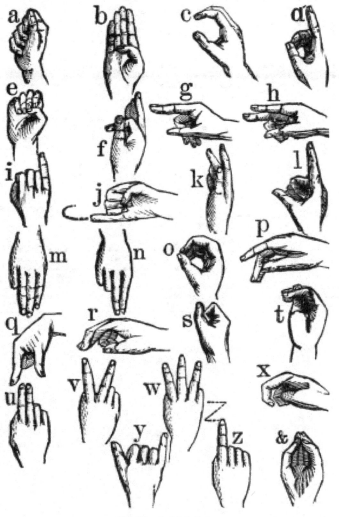

One-hand Alphabet.

• •

Latin Braille

ALFABETO DE LOS CIEGOS

LETRAS Y SIGNOS DE PUNTUACIÓN*

a	b	c	d	e	f	g	h	i	j	k	l
m	n	ñ	o	p	q	r	s	t	u	v	w
x	y	z	ch	ll	rr	á	é	í	ó	ú	ü

CIFRAS Y SIGNOS MATEMÁTICOS

numérico	1	2	3	4	5	6	7	8	9	0

* Los puntos gruesos representan los puntos en relieve; los otros sólo sirven para indicar en la figura la posición de los puntos en relieve en cada grupo.